UPDATES
on DSM-5
for Introductory Psychology

Matthew K. Nock
Harvard University

W9-ADJ-475

WORTH PUBLISHERS

A Macmillan Higher Education Company

Senior Vice President, Editorial and Production: Catherine Woods
Publisher: Kevin Feyen
Acquisitions Editor: Daniel DeBonis
Editorial Assistant: Katherine Garrett
Marketing Manager: Lindsay Johnson
Marketing Coordinator: Julie Tompkins
Senior Developmental Editor: Valerie Raymond
Director of Print and Digital Development: Tracey Kuehn
Associate Managing Editor: Lisa Kinne
Project Editor: Jennifer Bossert
Production Manager: Sarah Segal
Cover/Text Designer: Kevin Kall
Layout Designer: Linda Harms
Printing and Binding: RR Donnelley
Cover Art: Veer/Corbis

ISBN-13: 978-1-4641-6796-6
ISBN-10: 1-4641-6796-6

Printed in the United States of America

Worth Publishers
41 Madison Avenue
New York, NY 10010
www.worthpublishers.com

About the Author

Matthew K. Nock is Professor of Psychology and Director of the Laboratory for Clinical and Developmental Research at Harvard University. He received his BA from Boston University and his PhD in psychology from Yale University in 2003 and completed his clinical internship at Bellevue Hospital and the New York University Child Study Center. His research is aimed at advancing the understanding of why people behave in ways that are harmful to themselves, with an emphasis on suicide and other forms of self-harm. His research is multi-disciplinary in nature and uses a range of methodological approaches to better understand how these behaviors develop, how to predict them, and how to prevent their occurrence. His work has been recognized through the receipt of four early career awards from the American Psychological Association, the Association for Behavioral and Cognitive Therapies, and the American Association of Suicidology; in 2011 he was named a MacArthur Fellow. In addition to conducting research, he has been a consultant and scientific advisor to the National Institutes of Health, the World Health Organization's World Mental Health Survey Initiative, the American Psychological Association, and the American Psychiatric Association *DSM*–5 Childhood and Adolescent Disorder Work Group. At Harvard, he has received several teaching awards including the Roslyn Abramson Teaching Award and the Petra Shattuck Prize. In January 2014, he will join Daniel Schacter, Daniel Gilbert, and Daniel Wegner as a co-author of *Psychology, Third Edition.*

Preface

In May 2013, the American Psychiatric Association released the Fifth Edition of the *Diagnostic and Statistical Manual of Mental Disorders* (*DSM–5*), the manual that mental health professionals use to define and classify mental disorders. The new edition of our introductory textbook, *Psychology*, Third Edition (Schacter, Gilbert, Wegner, & Nock), available in January 2014, has been updated to accurately present the newest information included in *DSM–5*. In the meantime (i.e., for Fall 2013), we prepared this supplement to: (1) inform you about the most important changes in *DSM–5*, especially those that will affect material commonly presented in introduction to psychology courses, (2) share some ideas for how some of this material might be incorporated into your lectures, and (3) list places in the Second Edition of our book where material on mental disorders should be updated based on changes in *DSM–5*. We hope this information is helpful to you! Please feel free to contact Matthew Nock, PhD, at nock.matthew@gmail.com with any questions. Matt is joining us as a co-author for the Third Edition of this book. He is a clinical psychologist who is a professor of psychology at Harvard University and was a scientific advisor on *DSM–5*.

Good luck with your course!

Daniel L. Schacter

Daniel M. Wegner

Daniel T. Gilbert

Matthew K. Nock

Highlights of Changes in *DSM–5*

It has been 19 years since the last major revision to the *DSM*, so one would expect major changes to what is known about mental disorders, and as a result, to the manual used to diagnose and classify them. Although there have indeed been significant advances and resulting changes, many of which are described in the following pages, it is important to note that there is much more that is unchanged than changed. All of the disorders typically covered in introductory psychology courses—mood disorders, anxiety disorders, schizophrenia, dissociative disorders, and personality disorders—are still disorders. That being said, there are some important changes in *DSM–5* of which you should be aware. These changes are of two general types: (a) changes to the overall structure and approach of the manual that affect all disorders included, and (b) changes to individual disorders (e.g., changes in diagnostic criteria, reclassification as different type of disorder). Some of the most important of both types of changes are highlighted here. More extensive information about the changes to *DSM–5* can be found at the American Psychiatric Association's web site: http://psychiatry.org/practice/dsm/dsm5.

General Changes to the *DSM*

Removal of Multiaxial System

Perhaps the biggest change from *DSM–IV* to *DSM–5* is the removal of the multiaxial system. In *DSM–IV*, each mental disorder diagnosis included information on five axes: (Axis I) acute mental disorders, such as depression or schizophrenia; (Axis II) chronic mental disorders, such as personality disorder or mental retardation; (Axis III) medical or neurological conditions; (Axis IV) psychosocial stressors; and (Axis V) global assessment of functioning. In the past, every time an individual was assessed for the presence of a mental disorder, information about each of these five axes was recorded in his or her chart. That changes in the *DSM–5*. In an effort to bring the diagnosis of mental disorder in line with how medical conditions are diagnosed, diagnoses are considered to be present or absent (with no distinction among the former Axes I, II, or III); psychosocial and environmental problems are noted separately (now using the same *International Classification of Diseases* V and Z codes used in the diagnosis of medical conditions). Also consistent with the diagnosis of medical conditions, *DSM–5* separates the concept of disease or disorder from that of dysfunction, so Axis V is no longer included as part of the diagnosis of a mental disorder. If your biopsy indicates that you have cancer, you have cancer, regardless of whether that disease is impairing your daily activities. *DSM–5* is attempting to move in the same direction. The multiaxial system is presented in many introductory psychology textbooks, and this change may be one that requires attention in your course.

Removal of GAF

With the removal of Axis V (as noted before), so goes the Global Assessment of Functioning scale. This is the 0–100 scale used to rate an individual's current level of functioning. The rationale for dropping the GAF completely from *DSM–5* is that it had poor psychometric characteristics and lacked conceptual clarity (e.g., the 0–100 rating took into account a very broad range of factors such as clinical symptoms, suicide risk, and disabilities). Although the GAF has been removed from the *DSM–5*, the field continues to recognize the importance of assessing the presence of disability related to one's disorder, so the GAF has been replaced with a purer measure of disability: the World Health Organization Disability Assessment Schedule (WHODAS 2.0; a 36-item self-administered questionnaire that assesses illness-related disability over the past 30 days). Like the multiaxial system, the GAF is described in many introductory psychology textbooks, and this change may be another one that requires attention in your course.

Reorganization of Chapters

Rather than a change in material, this is a change in the order in which the different disorders are presented. Taking a developmental and life-span approach, the *DSM–5* first describes disorders believed to result from problems in development early in life (e.g., neurodevelopmental disorders), followed by disorders that typically develop during adolescence and young adulthood (e.g., depressive and bipolar disorders), followed by disorders that tend to occur in adulthood and older age (e.g., neurocognitive disorders). Beyond that, the *DSM–5* chapters (each of which describes a specific type of disorder) are organized based on symptom similarity and on recent advances in the understanding of the underlying vulnerabilities for mental disorders. For instance, the chapter on bipolar disorder sits between the chapters on schizophrenia spectrum disorders and depressive disorders because bipolar disorder shares symptoms with both of those types of disorders and because recent research has shown shared genetic vulnerabilities with those disorders.

Some Specific Changes to Individual Disorders

The specific changes to individual disorders in *DSM–5* are too numerous to list here. For a detailed list, go to the American Psychiatric Association's web site: http://psychiatry.org/practice/dsm/dsm5. However, here are some that affect the diagnoses typically covered in introductory psychology textbooks and courses.

Bipolar Disorder Is No Longer a Mood Disorder

Bipolar disorder was considered to be a mood disorder in *DSM–IV*, and is so classified in virtually all introductory psychology textbooks. In *DSM–5*, bipolar and related disorders (such as bipolar II disorder and cyclothymic disorder) are separated from mood disorders and, as noted above, sit between schizophrenia spectrum disorders and depressive disorders. The rationale for this change is twofold: (a) in addition to having major depressive episodes, people with bipolar disorder often experience psychotic symptoms, and (b) recent evidence from genetic and family studies show shared vulnerabilities for these disorders.

OCD and PTSD Are No Longer Anxiety Disorders

Obsessive-compulsive disorder (OCD) and post-traumatic stress disorder (PTSD) were both considered to be anxiety disorders in *DSM–IV* given that they involve fear and worry; however, each is now its own class of disorder due to recent advances in the understanding and conceptualization of these disorders. The new diagnostic category of obsessive-compulsive and related disorders includes OCD as well as hoarding disorder, trichotillomanic (hair-pulling) disorder, and body dysmorphic disorder. The new diagnostic category of trauma- and stressor-related disorders includes PTSD as well as adjustment disorder and reactive attachment disorder. Although this modification reflects a change in how these disorders are conceptualized by the field, these individual disorders generally are defined the same way in *DSM–5* as they were in *DSM–IV*.

Removal of the Bereavement Exclusion for Major Depressive Disorder

In describing major depressive disorder (MDD), many textbooks note that this disorder is different than the depressed mood that people experience following the death of a loved one. And in fact, *DSM–IV* included an exclusion for depressed mood in the context of bereavement (specifically, a person could be depressed for up to 2 months following the death of a loved one without being considered to have MDD). This "bereavement exclusion" has been removed in *DSM–5*. The reason for this change is that MDD typically occurs in the context of a psychosocial stressor, and bereavement is a psychosocial stressor and should be considered as such. Moreover, research suggests that bereavement-related depression typically occurs in those with a past history or family history of MDD, suggesting that it is not distinct from MDD. Although these are valid arguments, this modification has generated a great deal of debate both in scientific circles and the media.

Autism Spectrum Disorder

Another major change that has generated debate and controversy is the creation of autism spectrum disorder (ASD), a new category that represents a merging of four *DSM–IV* disorders: autistic disorder, Asperger's disorder, childhood disintegrative disorder, and pervasive developmental disorder not otherwise specified (and so these *DSM–IV* disorders are excluded from *DSM–5*). Proponents of this change argue that the new ASD represents a more reliable and scientifically valid category. However, the fact that field trials show that only about 90% of those with one of the *DSM–IV* disorders subsumed by ASD will meet criteria for this new disorder has led to a great deal of concern, especially among those receiving mental health services.

Ideas and Tips for Adapting Lectures

It can be difficult to keep up with all of the changes coming about in *DSM–5*, and even more difficult to know what information to present to students, and how best to do so. Here we share some ideas and tips for adapting your lectures on mental disorders. We hope you find them useful!

Present New Information on the Epidemiology of Mental Disorders

New epidemiological studies have provided valuable and easy-to-access information about mental disorders, including what percentage of people has them, who gets treated for them, and how their prevalence rates have changed over time (or in most cases, haven't changed over time). The prevalence of each mental disorder typically is included in introductory psychology texts; however, you can access much more information on them from epidemiological surveys conducted in the United States (from the National Comorbidity Survey: http://www.hcp.med.harvard.edu/ncs/) and around the world (from the World Mental Health Survey Initiative: http://www.hcp.med.harvard.edu/wmh/). With just a few clicks of a mouse, you can access data from these large-scale studies that can be used to plot out the rates of the different disorders in adolescents versus adults, men versus women, and so on. This information can serve as a really interesting launching point for discussions about mental disorders. Some key questions for discussion are:

- Why does the United States have higher rates of mental disorders than all other countries?
- Why are women more likely to have mood and anxiety disorders, whereas men are more likely to have impulse-control and substance use disorders?
- Why do most disorders increase so dramatically during adolescence and young adulthood?

Information on the epidemiology of mental disorders can provide a great jump start for rich discussions about these problems.

Pull Back the Curtain on How Diagnoses Are Made

With all of this talk about how mental disorders are defined in *DSM–5* a natural questions in the minds of many students (and perhaps instructors!) are: How are diagnoses actually assigned? How do clinicians decide if a person has a mental disorder or not? Researchers and clinicians often make determinations about which disorders a person may meet criteria for using a structured clinical interview. These interviews essentially convert the *DSM* criteria for each disorder into a series of interview questions. For instance, given that a person must have at least five of the nine symptoms of MDD to qualify for this diagnosis, the MDD section of structured clinical interviews typically has nine questions about depression (one per symptom), and the clinician asks each of these items and makes a determination about whether that person meets criteria for that disorder. There are a number of clinical interviews available in the literature (and on the web), such as the MINI International Neuropsychiatric Interview (MINI, for adults) and the Kiddie—Schedule for Affective Disorders and Schizophrenia

(K-SADS, for children and adolescents). Although these interviews should not be given to students for diagnosing themselves and those around them (as they are meant to be used by licensed clinicians), it could be instructive and informative to describe structured clinical interviews to students both to demystify the diagnostic process, and to generate discussions about the reliability and validity of using self-reported information to arrive at diagnoses of mental disorders. This is an issue that is touched on briefly in many introductory texts, and the incorporation of information about how diagnoses are actually made could help to deepen the discussion of this important issue. Some key questions for discussion are:

- How reliable and valid is the information that clinicians obtain from clinical interviews?

- What other sources of information should clinicians consider when diagnosing a mental disorder?

- When making diagnoses in clinical practice, most clinicians do not make use of clinical interviews such as those described above, and instead ask their own questions in an attempt to determine an individual's diagnosis. What are the potential problems with this approach?

Discuss Some of the Current Controversies Surrounding *DSM–5*

Over the years, many have referred to the *DSM* as the "bible" of mental disorders. Any time someone tries to change the bible, people are sure to get upset. However, the development of *DSM–5* has been especially contentious and chock full of controversy. For instance, the American Psychiatric Association states that the development of *DSM–5* has been an open and transparent process; however, critics note that much of the revising has been done behind closed doors by scientists required to sign confidentiality agreements. The American Psychiatric Association notes that all of the changes to mental disorders in *DSM–5* are based on scientific research; however, critics suggest that some may be driven by the influence of pharmaceutical companies looking to make more money from drug sales. Interestingly, one of the most outspoken critics has been Allen Frances, M.D., who was the chair of the *DSM–IV* Task Force. His blog at *Psychology Today*, "DSM–5 in Distress" (http://www.psychologytoday.com/blog/dsm5-in-distress), is a wonderful place to read an insider's perspective on some of the biggest controversies surrounding *DSM–5*, many of which are sure to generate thoughtful classroom discussion about key issues regarding mental disorders and their diagnosis. Some potential questions for discussion are:

- Currently, decisions about how disorders in the *DSM* are classified and defined are made by a committee of scientific experts. What are the strengths and weaknesses of this approach?

- Does removing the bereavement exclusion for major depressive disorder result in more accurate diagnostic criteria, or the pathologizing of normal grief?

- The new definition of autism spectrum disorder eliminates the category of Asperger's disorder and causes approximately 10% of those people currently diagnosed with an autism spectrum disorder to no longer meet diagnostic criteria. Is this a good outcome, because these people are no longer considered to have a diagnosis? Or a bad outcome, because these people may be in danger of losing health services for their condition?

Introduce the Research Domain Criteria Project (RDoC)

Although much of the current attention in the field and in the media has been on *DSM–5*, the most recent scientific and media attention (and controversy) have focused on what is now on the horizon: the Research Domain Criteria Project (RDoC). RDoC is a new initiative developed by the National Institute of Mental Health (NIMH) that aims to guide the classification and understanding of mental disorders by revealing the basic processes that give rise to them. Rather than thinking about and defining mental disorders as collections of symptoms (as currently done in the *DSM*), RDoC aims to reveal the biological and behavioral causes of psychopathology and to classify and define disorders based on that new scientific understanding. The RDoC is not intended to immediately replace the *DSM*, but to inform future revisions in the coming years. Succinctly characterizing the issue, Thomas Insel, Director of the NIMH, noted that, although many people describe the *DSM* as a bible, it is more accurate to think of it like a dictionary that provides labels and current definitions. As he stated in a recent *New York Times* article: "People think that everything has to match *DSM* criteria, but you know what? Biology never read that book."[1] The RDoC approach is expected to transform the way we think about mental disorders, and no doubt will be included in introductory and abnormal psychology textbooks in the years ahead. In the meantime, you can read about this approach at the NIMH web site (http://www.nimh.nih.gov/research-funding/rdoc/index.shtml), where you can find information and links that you can share with students to introduce them to what is likely to be the future of mental disorders. Some potential discussion questions in this area are:

- What are the strengths and weaknesses of defining mental disorders based on their underlying biological causes?

- Look at the Research Domain Criteria; which chapters of your book do you see represented in these different domains?

[1]Belluck, P., & Benedict, C. (2013, May 7). Psychiatry's new guide falls short, experts say. *The New York Times*, p. A13.

Updates on *DSM–5* for *Psychology,* Second Edition

Chapter 14: Psychological Disorders

(a) Of course, references to *DSM–IV* are now slightly outdated given the publication of *DSM–5*.

 Suggestion: Inform students of the recent publication of *DSM–5*, and that you will note where information has changed.

(b) Table 14.1 (Main *DSM–IV–TR* Categories of Mental Disorders, p. 553) is now slightly out of date, as disorder categories have changed slightly in *DSM–5*.

 Suggestion: Refer students to the link to updated information on Worth Publishers' web site: www.worthpublishers.com/dsm5update/sgwn

(c) Table 14.2 (Global Assessment of Functioning [GAF] Scale, p. 555) is now out of date, as the GAF has been dropped from *DSM–5*.

 Suggestion: Consider discussing the reasons for this change.

(d) Table 14.3 (Types of Schizophrenia, p. 576) is now out of date, as these have been dropped from *DSM–5* due to concerns about reliability and validity of these distinctions.

 Suggestion: Inform students of this change, and perhaps discuss it as a concrete example of how the conceptualization and classification of mental disorders change in response to scientific findings (i.e., if something lacks reliability and validity, it is removed from the system).

(e) Anxiety disorders: Obsessive-compulsive disorder (OCD, pp. 563–564) was an anxiety disorder in *DSM–IV–TR* but is now its own class of disorder in *DSM–5*, as noted earlier.

 Suggestion: Discuss the similarities and differences between OCD and the anxiety disorders. The placement of OCD at the end of the anxiety disorder section provides a potential opportunity to talk about the fact that OCD is now considered to be distinct from the other anxiety disorders.

(f) Mood disorders (pp. 564–571): This category has been split in two in *DSM–5*: depressive disorders, and bipolar and related disorders.

 Suggestion: Discuss the fact that although both depressive disorders and bipolar disorders involve depressed mood, recent research showing overlap between bipolar and psychotic disorders has led to the acknowledgement that bipolar disorder is distinct from depressive disorder and not merely a disorder of mood. The fact that depressive and bipolar disorders are described in different subsections in *Psychology*, Second Edition, and that the schizophrenia section follows soon after, provides a nice setup for discussing this change.

(g) Depressive disorders: The Second Edition notes that major depressive disorder is "different from the normal responses of sorrow and grief that accompany a tragic situation such as the death of a loved one" (p. 565). This is no longer true given the removal of the bereavement exclusion in *DSM–5*.

Suggestion: Talk with students about this change, which has generated a great deal of debate among researchers, clinicians, and the public. Is it a change they support? Does it pathologize normal grieving?

(h) Dissociative disorders: Dissociative amnesia and dissociative fugue (p. 573) are no longer separate diagnoses, as in *DSM–IV*. Instead, dissociative fugue is now a subtype of dissociative amnesia in *DSM–5*.

Suggestion: Consider discussing this with students. Given the rarity of dissociative disorders, this change has generated much less debate and discussion than changes to mood and anxiety disorders.

(i) Hot Science box (p. 577): Mental retardation is now called intellectual disability, and autistic disorder and Asperger's disorder are now combined into an autism spectrum disorder (ASD) diagnosis in *DSM–5*.

Suggestion: These disorders are mentioned only in this box and not in the text, so there is flexibility in how much you discuss these particular changes. Notably, both of these changes, especially the modification to ASD, have gotten a great deal of scientific and media attention, and may be something worth discussing with students.

Chapters 15 and 16: Treatment of Psychological Disorders, and Stress and Health

Psychology, Second Edition, is accurate and up-to-date regarding the information presented on mental disorders in these chapters.

Updates on *DSM–5* for *Introducing Psychology*, Second Edition
Chapter 13: Psychological Disorders

(a) Of course, references to *DSM–IV* are now slightly outdated given the publication of *DSM–5*. *Suggestion*: Inform students of the recent publication of *DSM–5*, and that you will note where information has changed.

(b) Table 13.1 (Main *DSM–IV–TR* Categories of Mental Disorders, p. 408) is now slightly out of date, as disorder categories have changed slightly in *DSM–5*.

Suggestion: Refer students to the link to updated information on Worth Publishers' web site: www.worthpublishers.com/dsm5update/sgwn

(c) Anxiety disorders: Obsessive-compulsive disorder (OCD, p. 416) was an anxiety disorder in *DSM–IV–TR*, but is now its own class of disorder in *DSM–5*, as noted earlier.

Suggestion: Discuss the similarities and differences between OCD and the anxiety disorders. The placement of OCD at the end of the anxiety disorder section provides a potential opportunity to talk about the fact that OCD is now considered to be distinct from the other anxiety disorders.

(d) Mood disorders (pp. 417–421): This category has been split in two in *DSM–5*: depressive disorders, and bipolar and related disorders.

   Suggestion: Discuss the fact that although both depressive disorders and bipolar disorders involve depressed mood, recent research showing overlap between bipolar and psychotic disorders has led to the acknowledgement that bipolar disorder is distinct from depressive disorder and not merely a disorder of mood. The fact that depressive and bipolar disorders are described in different subsections in *Introducing Psychology*, Second Edition, and that the schizophrenia section follows soon after, provides a nice setup for discussing this change.

(e) Depressive disorders: The Second Edition notes that major depressive disorder is "different from the normal responses of sorrow and grief that accompany a tragic situation such as the death of a loved one" (p. 417). This is no longer true given the removal of the bereavement exclusion in *DSM–5*.

   Suggestion: Talk with students about this change, which has generated a great deal of debate among researchers, clinicians, and the public. Is it a change they support? Does it pathologize normal grieving?

(f) Dissociative disorders: Dissociative amnesia and dissociative fugue (pp. 422–423) are no longer separate diagnoses as in *DSM–IV*. Instead, dissociative fugue is now a subtype of dissociative amnesia in *DSM–5*.

   Suggestion: Consider discussing this with students. Given the rarity of dissociative disorders, this change has generated much less debate and discussion than changes to mood and anxiety disorders.

(g) Hot Science box (p. 425): Mental retardation is now called intellectual disability, and autistic disorder and Asperger's disorder are now combined into an autism spectrum disorder (ASD) diagnosis in *DSM–5*.

   Suggestion: These disorders are mentioned only in this box and not in the text, so there is flexibility in how much you discuss these particular changes. Notably, both of these changes, especially the modification to ASD, have gotten a great deal of scientific and media attention, and may be something worth discussing with students.

Chapters 14 and 15: Treatment of Psychological Disorders, and Stress and Health

Introducing Psychology, Second Edition, is accurate and up-to-date regarding the information presented on mental disorders in these chapters.

Index